CONTENTS

"I take charge of plays on the court. With *NBA Slam & Jam Study Skills*, you'll take charge of your study skills. You'll score big in the classroom and in life!"

John Stockton of the Utah Jazz

Get On Schedule!

NBA players lead busy lives. Just ask New York Knick Patrick Ewing. Besides playing 82 NBA games a year, he does charity work and makes commercials. He also lifts weights and practices his patented jump shot. Last, but not least, he loves spending time with his family.

How does such a busy man fit all these things into his life? It's easy. He organizes his time.

Organizing your time means figuring out when you are going to do what each day. If you organize your time well, you won't find yourself frantically starting your homework fifteen minutes before bed. You'll never be late for class. And you'll have plenty of time to do the things you love.

Schedules are a great way to organize your time. They can help you plan your day, your week, or even your whole year! A schedule helps you tell at a glance where to go or what to do next. So what are you waiting for? Get going and learn about schedules by doing the exercises on the next three pages.

AMAZING NBA FACT

Patrick Ewing has scored over 21,000 points in his 12-year career— more than any other Knick!

Patrick Ewing

Reading a Schedule

Patrick Ewing uses a schedule to organize his time. Take a look at his sample schedule on this page. Notice how he has found time to include all of the things that are important to him. By sticking to his schedule, Patrick has plenty of time for himself and his family!

Use the schedule to answer the questions below.

MONDAY	TUESDAY	WEDNESDAY	THURSDAY	FRIDAY	SATURDAY	SUNDAY
7am Guest: radio talk	7am	7am	7am	7am	7am	7am
8am show	8am Meeting with	8am	8am Team Doctor:	8am Team Meeting	8am Fly to New York	8am
9am	9am agent	9am Guest Speaker:	9am check-up	9am Light Practice	9am	9am
10am	10am	10am Roosevelt High School	10am	10am	10am	10am Gym: weight
11am Watch Chicago	11am Gym: weight	11am	11am	11am	11am ESPN Interview	11am training
12pm Bulls films	12pm training	12pm	12pm	12pm Gym: weight	12pm	12pm
1pm	1pm	1pm Interview: New York Times	1pm Fly to Boston	1pm training	1pm	1pm
2pm	2pm	2pm	2pm	2pm	2pm	2pm
3pm Press Conference	3pm	3pm Gym: weight training	3pm	3pm	3pm Gym: weight training	3pm Charity Event
4pm Light Practice	4pm	4pm	4pm Light Practice	4pm	4pm	4pm
5pm	5pm Pre-Game Meeting	5pm	5pm	5pm Pre-Game Meeting	5pm	5pm Pre-Game Meeting
6pm	6pm Pre-game Warm-Up	6pm TV News Interview	6pm Team Dinner	6pm Pre-game Warm-Up	6pm TV News Interview	6pm Pre-game Warm-Up
7pm	7pm Game: Chicago Bulls	7pm	7pm	7pm Game: Boston Celtics	7pm	7pm Game: Utah Jazz

1. How many games does Patrick Ewing have this week?____________________

2. What will Patrick be doing at:

a. 3 p.m. Monday?____________________

b. 9 a.m. Tuesday?____________________

3. How many nights this week will Patrick be in Boston?____________________

4. Can Patrick add the following to his schedule:

a. A 45-minute radio interview at 8:30 a.m. Wednesday?____________________

b. A players meeting at 1 p.m. Tuesday?____________________

c. Volunteering at a homeless shelter early on Sunday morning?____________________

5. How much time does Patrick have:

a. between his speaking engagement on Wednesday and his interview?____________________

b. between weight training and the pre-game meeting on Friday?____________________

6. If Patrick wanted to take a yoga class three days a week from 1:00 to 2:00 p.m., which days could he do it?____________________

Creating a Schedule

Look at this computer printout of a student's classes. It's pretty easy to read, right? Sure. But it could be even easier to remember and follow if it was organized neatly on a schedule. Take the information from the list and put it on the blank schedule below. If you need help, use Patrick's schedule on page 3 as a model.

Take the information from the list and put it on the blank schedule below.

Band Practice	2:20	M
Driver's Ed	8:10	MW
English	12:55	MTWThF
Health	12:10	TTh
History	9:10	MTWThF
Homeroom	8:55	MTWThF
Intramurals	2:20	ThF
Lunch	11:25 12:10	TTh, MWF
Math	9:55	MTWThF
Phys Ed	11:25	MWF
Science	1:40	MTWThF
Shop	10:40	MWF
Spanish	8:10	TThF
Study Hall	10:40	TTh

Time	MONDAY	TUESDAY	WEDNESDAY	THURSDAY	FRIDAY
8:10–8:50a.m.					
8:55–9:05					
9:10–9:50					
9:55–10:35					
10:40–11:20					
11:25–12:05p.m.					
12:10–12:50					
12:55–1:35					
1:40–2:20					
2:20–5:00					

1. Which is easier to follow, the list or the schedule? Why? How might creating a schedule like the one above, help you get to class on time?

____

____

____

Time Management

What's the key to managing your time efficiently? You need to make good choices. That means figuring out what you *need* to do, what you *want* to do, and what it's *possible* to do with the time you have.

Sharon wants to sign up for some activities after school. The choices on the list below all interest her. Help her choose activities and create a manageable schedule by answering some of the following questions.

AFTER-SCHOOL ACTIVITIES

Drama Club: MWF 2:30-4:00
Band: TTH 3:00-4:30
Student Volunteers for the Environment: Th 3:30-4:30
Junior Varsity Basketball Practice: MTWF 3:30-5:00
Junior Varsity Volleyball Practice: MTWTh 3:00-4:30
Chess Club: MF 2:30-3:30
Pottery: TTh 2:30-3:30
School Newspaper: MThF 2:30-4:30

1. Which activities meet on Tuesday and Thursday afternoons?

____

____

2. Could Sharon do both Drama Club and Junior Varsity Basketball? Why, or why not?

____

____

3. Choose three activities and fill in Sharon's afterschool schedule. Make sure the three activities meet the following requirements:

a. Sharon wants to play a sport.
b. Sharon needs to keep Wednesday free from 2:30-3:30 for homework help.
c. Sharon wants to find time to do either Drama Club or Pottery.

Sharon's Afterschool Schedule

TIME	MONDAY	TUESDAY	WEDNESDAY	THURSDAY	FRIDAY
2:30			HOMEWORK HELP ↕		
3:00					
3:30					
4:00					
4:30					
5:00					

On Your Own

On a separate piece of paper, draw a blank schedule exactly like the one Patrick used on page 3. First, fill in the things you do at the same time each day, like your classes and having dinner. Then, add things you need do every day, but not necessarily at a particular time, like your homework. Finally, fill in the time left with fun activities!

Write it Down

Glen Rice of the Charlotte Hornets

Believe it or not, NBA players spend a lot of time studying. What do they study? Each other. Before two teams meet on the court, each one studies the other team's moves, either live or on film. How do players remember what they observe about their opponents? They take notes.

Taking notes means recording information on paper. If you take notes on new information you hear or read, you'll be able to go back and review them anytime you forget something. In school, notes are useful when you're writing a paper, doing your homework, or studying for a test. At other times, taking notes is a great way to record something you don't want to forget.

But your notes will only be useful if you take good ones. Taking good notes requires careful listening and close reading. Good notes are organized, not scrawled all over the page. Important points or facts are emphasized by being underlined, starred, or circled. Each set of related facts gets its own line or paragraph. To take good notes, follow these steps.

1. As you read or listen, decide which ideas and details are important. Do this by asking yourself questions like: "Who or what is the subject?" "What happened?" "Why?" "When and where did it happen?"
2. Give each new idea or event a new paragraph. Group related details together.
3. Keep your notes neat and organized! Don't use sloppy handwriting. Messy notes are hard to understand when you review them later. Good, clearly written, notes can be understood by everyone.

AMAZING NBA FACT

In the 1996-97 season, Glen Rice made 47 percent of his three-point shots, a career high!

Taking Notes from Articles

Look at these notes an NBA player took while reading about a game between the Charlotte Hornets and the Golden State Warriors. The tips in yellow tell you why this player's notes are clear and easy to follow.

The player circled the points each team scored so he could see at a glance who won the game.

The player underlined key information that helps him remember that the Hornets are a hot team these days.

Hornets	Warriors
points: 100	points: 93
game went into OT	*Joe Smith—31 pts, 15 reb.!
Vlade Divac—10 pts, 12 reb. 9 assts	Latrell Sprewell—9 assts
Mason injured—not playing	Turnovers: 17
Won 10th time in 12 games	

The player starred important information about Joe Smith's great performance. That tells him Joe's a player to watch!

Now it's your turn. Read the brief newspaper article below about a game. As you read, take notes in the columns about each team following the example above. Don't forget to star, circle, and underline important points. We've done the first example for you.

Bulls Win Again

CHICAGO -- Behind Scottie Pippen's 26 points and Michael Jordan's 23, the Chicago Bulls defeated the Detroit Pistons for the 19th consecutive time last night, with a 96-87 overtime victory in the United Center.

Returning from a hamstring injury, Chicago center Luc Longley added 16 points and 12 rebounds. Dennis Rodman grabbed 18 rebounds helping the Bulls to a 42 - 25 rebounding advantage over the Pistons.

The Pistons, playing their fifth game in seven nights, got 16 points from Grant Hill, but he shot just 5-of-14 from the field and was 6-of-11 from the free-throw line.

Bulls	Pistons
points: 96	points: 87

STUDY

Revising Notes

Take **note:** I'm taking it to the **basket!**

Here are some notes a different NBA player took while listening to a Lakers-Jazz game on the radio. He was in a hurry, so he didn't take very good notes. Can you help him out by revising them? Revising notes is a good way to study because it helps you remember information later. First, put the notes below in order by sorting and organizing the information by team. Then write your revised notes on the blank notebook paper on this page. Use the steps at left to help you.

Utah Jazz Karl Malone

1. List details under each team title.
2. Shorten sentences and phrases, if possible.
3. Delete unimportant details.
4. Underline, circle, or star important facts where neccessary.
5. Make sure notes are written neatly and clearly.

PLAYER NOTES

Lakers lead 30-26 in first quarter. Karl Malone has a great slam dunk that makes crowd roar. Elden Campbell blocks a shot.

John Stockton makes two three-point shots in a row. Jazz lead at the half, 55-49.

Jazz win: 108-103.

Jones misses some important free throws down the stretch.

Eddie Jones has a beautiful lay up.

Jazz starters: Karl Malone, John Stockton, Greg Ostertag, Byron Russell, Jeff Hornacek.

Lakers starters: Shaquille O'Neal, Eddie Jones, Nick Van Exel, Elden Campbell, Robert Horry.

Robert Horry misses a shot.

Shaq blocks Greg Ostertag's shot.

Karl Malone finishes with 36 points and 12 rebounds.

The Jazz take a 2-1 lead in the playoff series.

REVISED NOTES

Lakers

Jazz

Writing Paragraphs from Notes

1. Karl Malone
Forward
34 years old, 6-9, 256 pounds
Plays for the Utah Jazz
12th NBA season
10th-leading scorer in NBA history
Named to All-NBA First Team for nine straight seasons
MVP in 1997
* strong and powerful, players hate to defend him in the post
Named one of NBA's 50 greatest players

2. Penny Hardaway
Guard
26 years old, 6-7, 200 pounds
Plays for the Orlando Magic
4th NBA season
Named to 1995 and 1996 All-NBA First Team
*Helped Magic reach the 1995 NBA finals
Makes spectacular passes and shots
Explosive scorer, recorded back-to-back 40-point games in 97 playoffs

3. Shaquille O'Neal
Center
25 years old, 7-1, 301 pounds
Plays for the Los Angeles Lakers
5th NBA season
1993 Rookie of the Year
Led NBA in scoring in 1994-95
Named one of NBA's 50 greatest players
Very big and strong, virtually unstoppable in the lane

Often, people must write school papers or paragraphs from notes they have taken earlier. For them, it's important to take good notes because they need to make sense of them later. Here are some notes that an NBA scout took about some of the league's biggest stars. Organize the information in the right order, then use the notes to write a paragraph about each player. Pay special attention to things that are underlined, circled, or starred. We've done one example for you.

1. Karl Malone plays forward for the Utah Jazz. He's 34 years old, 6 feet 9 inches tall and weighs 256 pounds. Other players hate to defend Karl in the post because he's so powerful. In his 12-year career, Karl has earned lots of awards, including the 1997 MVP award. He's the 10th leading scorer in NBA history and has been named to the All-NBA First Team for nine straight seasons. He was named one of the NBA's 50 greatest players.

2. ______________________________

3. ______________________________

On Your Own

Read a sports article and take notes, then give your notes to a friend or a classmate. See if he or she can write a paragraph using the details from your notes.

Inform Yourself!

Basketball players like to keep informed. So, when Grant Hill picks up the sports section during basketball season, he reads carefully. He wants to find out as much as possible about other players and teams. He also wants to remember what he finds out later.

Fortunately, Grant knows how to find and remember important information when he reads. He uses a pen so he can underline big ideas and details. He knows how to read charts, graphs, and diagrams, and pays close attention to the information they display. Later, he can look back at what he's underlined to review what's important to know.

You can follow Grant's example when you read, especially when you read for school. Underlining important ideas and details will help you remember them better. Learning how to read information that is presented in different ways, such as charts and diagrams, can also help you. Get some practice being a careful reader with the exercises on the next three pages.

AMAZING NBA FACT

Grant Hill was the first rookie ever to lead the balloting for the All-Star Game with 1,289,585 votes in 1995.

Grant Hill of the Detroit Pistons

Reading Texts

Texts are printed reading material. Newspaper and magazine articles are texts. So are essays, stories, and books. What's the best way to read texts? Try using a pen, pencil, or highlighter to underline important details and pieces of information. But before you underline, make sure the text belongs to you. You don't want to destroy a school or library book.

Highlighting texts helps you in two ways. First, underlining details as you read helps you remember them later. Second, when you need to review for a test or an assignment, the most important information will be easy to spot quickly.

Now try it yourself. Read the steps in the left margin. Then underline the important points in this article about Detroit Pistons star Grant Hill. We've underlined one example for you.

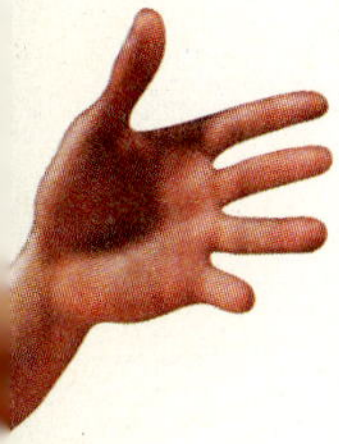

1. Who or what is the article about? Always underline the subject of what you're reading, whether it's a basketball player or the American Revolution.

2. When did things happen? Underline any dates you see as you read. You never know when you'll want to refer to them later. Also underline the information the dates refer to.

3. What is the most important thing the article is saying about its subject? Underline any phrases that state or point to the article's main idea.

THE RIGHT STUFF

Grant Hill has played eye-popping games for the Detroit Pistons ever since he entered the league in 1994. In 1996-97, he led the NBA with 13 triple-doubles. "When Grant plays great, we're an awfully good team," Pistons coach Doug Collins says.

When Grant came out of Duke University, he was looking to fit in with the rest of the Pistons, nothing more. It bothered him that because he had helped lead Duke to two NCAA championships, people expected him to become a leader and transform the Pistons overnight. Always shy growing up, being a leader wasn't a role that came easily to Grant.

It all changed after the 1996 Olympics, though. Being a member of the 1996 Dream Team convinced Grant that he had the ability and personality to take charge of the Pistons.

"Here are the guys I always looked up to, and now I'm playing with them," Grant says. "I said, 'Hey, this is the NBA's best. If I can play with Scottie Pippen every day, I can play with anybody.' " Hill's no longer a reluctant leader.

Now use what you've underlined to help you answer these questions. If you can't find the answers in what you've already underlined, read the article again and underline the answers when you find them.

1. When did Grant Hill enter the league? ____________________

2. Why did Grant have trouble being a leader? ____________________

3. When did it all change for Grant? ____________________

____

Interpreting a Chart

Sometimes information isn't presented in words and sentences. Instead, it can be shown in a chart. Charts are a way of presenting information visually. They can make information easier to see at a glance. They can also be a way to pack a lot of information into a small space. A chart can show information that might take many pages of text to describe.

One common chart that many basketball fans read is a box score. A box score gives statistics from a particular game. Take a look at the box score below. The tips in yellow will show you how to read it.

1. The first thing you should read on any chart or graph is the title. That tells you what the chart is about. The two titles below are team names. They tell you which team's stats are being shown.

2. Next, look at the top, sides, and bottom. These labels will tell you what information is being shown on the chart. This box score has players' names down one side, and different stats across the top. So, you can tell that it's showing you the individual stats for each player. Look at the rest of the tips to find out what these stats are.

HAWKS

	Min.	FG	FT	R	A	PF	Pts.
Corbin	40	5-11	0-0	5	6	2	14
Laettner	43	8-13	2-2	4	2	5	18
Mutombo	37	5-9	7-8	7	1	3	17
Smith	47	10-19	1-3	6	1	4	22
Blaylock	44	3-12	0-0	9	7	2	7
Henderson	9	0-1	2-2	1	0	2	2
Recasner	15	0-3	0-0	2	1	0	0
Lauderdale	1	0-1	0-0	0	0	0	0
James	3	0-1	0-0	0	0	2	0
Newbill	1	0-0	0-0	0	0	0	0
Totals	240	31-70	12-15	34	18	20	80

PISTONS

	Min.	FG	FT	R	A	PF	Pts.
Hill	37	7-19	11-13	5	3	5	25
Thorpe	22	5-9	2-2	8	2	3	12
Mills	40	3-8	0-0	6	1	4	7
Dumars	44	5-13	1-1	4	0	3	12
Hunter	39	5-10	0-0	2	1	1	13
McKie	26	3-5	0-0	3	2	2	7
Long	32	4-7	9-9	6	2	2	17
Totals	240	32-71	23-25	34	11	20	93

3. This tells you how many **minutes** each player played.

4. These tell you about **field goals.** The first number shows how many a player made. The second number shows how many a player attempted.

5. This tells you how many **rebounds** a player got.

6. This tells you how many **assists** a player had.

7. This tells you how many **personal fouls** a player committed.

8. This tells you how many **points** a player scored.

9. This tells you how many **free throws** a player made and attempted.

Now that you know how to read a chart, try answering the questions below. Underline, in the box score, information you used to answer each question.

1. What team won the game? ______________________________

2. Who scored the most points? ______________________________

3. Which two players got the fewest rebounds? ______________________________

4. Which player had the most assists? ______________________________

ant Hill of the Detroit Pistons battles Dikembe
tombo of the Atlanta Hawks

On Your Own

Look for charts and graphs as you read. Underline important information you find in them. Read more basketball box scores in your newspaper, then go back and answer the questions on page 12 for each one.

Following a Diagram

Diagrams are drawings that show and explain objects or events. Every NBA player knows how to follow diagrams. That's because when coaches call time-outs, they often draw diagrams of plays. If players can't read these diagrams, they won't know where to go on the basketball court. A coach drew the diagram below to show his team how to pass the ball to the open player for a game-winning shot. Use diagram labels to help you understand it.

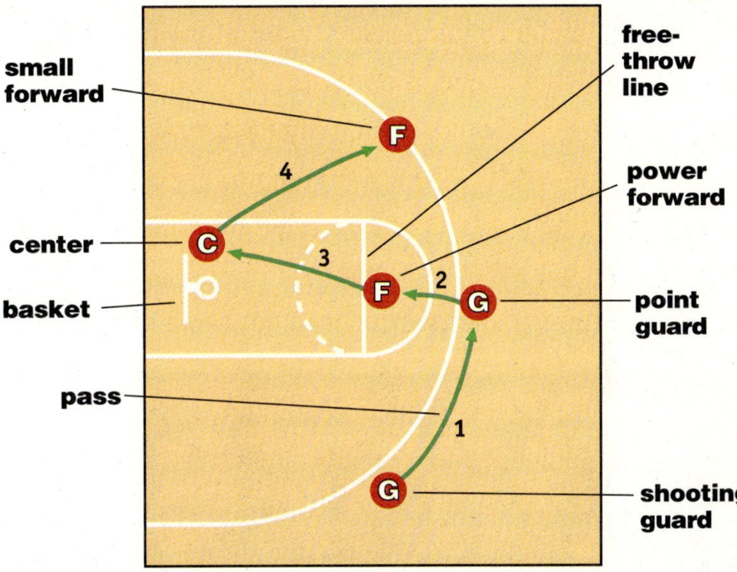

Use the diagram to answer these questions.

1. Which player is standing on the free-throw line?

____

2. Which player is next to the basket?

____

3. Which player makes the first pass?

____

4. Which player makes the fourth pass?

____

5. Which player takes the shot?

____

Look it up!

Wayne Coffey

Wayne Coffey is a sportswriter. You'll find his articles in magazines and newspapers all over the country. For Wayne, having the right facts and information is crucial to his success.

"Writers face deadlines," explains Coffey. "I need to have dates, stats, words, and a ton of research right at my fingertips."

Let's say that Wayne is about to sit down and write an article about Seattle SuperSonics guard Gary Payton. Where will he get the information he needs? Where will he go to check the spelling of a word? What if he wants to put an interesting fact about Seattle, Washington into his opening paragraph? Where will he get his information?

Wayne (or any sportswriter) can get some of this information from a sports media guide. Or, he could find out what he needs in reference books like the dictionary, almanac, and encyclopedia.

Seattle SuperSonic Gary Payton and Houston Rocket Hakeem Olajuwon

Knowing how to use reference books will help you in school. Reference materials can help you find the answer to a question, the meaning of a word, or the facts you need to complete an assignment. And, just like Wayne, you may find that reference materials can also be helpful to you in your future career. The activities on the following pages will give you some practice with these reference materials.

AMAZING NBA FACT

Gary Payton has only missed 2 out of 574 games in his seven-year career!

Using an Almanac

Quick! Do you know the answers to these questions?

What's the address for the Denver Nuggets basketball team?

Who was voted MVP in 1984, 1985, and 1986?

Which player did the Milwaukee Bucks draft in 1997?

If you don't already know, where would you find the answers to these questions? In the almanac, of course!

An almanac has one job to do: Provide you with the most up-to-date information on thousands of topics. To use an almanac, go to the index. Unlike most books, an almanac puts its index in the front, not the back.

To help you, each main index heading is printed in heavy type and listed in alphabetical order. Some headings have several sections listed to help you figure out exactly which pages might contain the information you need.

Look at the excerpt from an almanac index above. Where would you turn to in order to answer the questions at the top of this page?

General Index

-B-

Use an almanac from your classroom, library, or home to answer the questions below. (Warning: Your answers could differ from your classmates depending on which year your almanac was written.)

Title of almanac you are using:

____

Year the almanac is covering:

____

1. What is the population of Oakland, California?

____

2. On what page will you find a list of baseball teams in the National League?

____

3a. Where is the deepest lake in the United States?________________________

b. How deep is it?________________________

4. On what page will you find the national flag of Poland? ________________________

5. Who won the 1976 presidential election?

____

6. What is the name of the tallest building in the United States?

____

Lesson 4 continued on page 18 ☛

Terrell Brandon of the Cleveland Cavaliers takes it to the hoop!

Dear Parent,

Welcome to *NBA Slam & Jam Study Skills*! This workbook has been designed with basketball fans in mind. It uses the NBA stars kids love to teach study skills that are essential for school success and important to everyday life. As your child completes the workbook, you can actively participate in the learning process by following some of these tips:

- Go over each lesson with your child. When your child has completed a lesson, ask him or her to explain what the lesson was about and what was learned.

- Look for opportunities, such as the suggestions below, in which your child can use the study skills taught in this book.
  - **a.** Ask your child to create a schedule for weekend activities or holiday school breaks.
  - **b.** Ask your child to underline important information in an article from a newspaper or magazine. Then read the article and underline what you would consider important information. Compare and contrast both versions with your child.
  - **c.** Help your child select a topic and five facts he or she would like to research about that topic. Then have your child use various reference books, such as dictionaries, encyclopedias or almanacs to find out the information.

- Bring home a bus or a train timetable. Then have your child choose an imaginary time he or she wants to travel. Ask your child to interpret the chart for the right departure and arrival information.

- Encourage your child to write down some keywords he or she would use to find out more about a subject, such as a favorite sport, hobby, actor/actress, or musician. Then have your child conduct a web search using those keywords. If you don't have access to the Internet, try your local library. Help your child modify his or her keywords to conduct a successful search.

We hope you and your child enjoy using *NBA Slam & Jam Study Skills*. See the back of this guide for other *NBA Slam & Jam Skills* workbooks, which provide practice in different subject areas.

—The Editors

SLAM & JAM STUDY SKILLS (Grades 6–8)

ANSWER KEY

Page 3: **1.** three games **2a.** Attending a press conference **2b.** Meeting with agent **3.** one night **4a.** no **4b.** yes **4c.** yes **5a.** one hour **5b.** three hours **6.** Monday, Tuesday, Saturday, or Sunday.

Page 4:

	Monday	**Tuesday**	**Wednesday**	**Thursday**	**Friday**
8:10-8:50	Driver's Ed.	Spanish	Driver's Ed.	Spanish	Spanish
8:55-9:05	Homeroom	Homeroom	Homeroom	Homeroom	Homeroom
9:10-9:50	History	History	History	History	History
9:55-10:35	Math	Math	Math	Math	Math
10:40-11:20	Shop	Study Hall	Shop	Study Hall	Shop
11:25-12:05	Phys. Ed	Lunch	Phys. Ed	Lunch	Phys. Ed
12:10-12:50	Lunch	Health	Lunch	Health	Lunch
12:55-1:35	English	English	English	English	English
1:40-2:20	Science	Science	Science	Science	Science
2:20-5:00	Band Practice			Intramurals	Intramurals

1. Answers will vary but students should recognize that the schedule is easier to follow than the list because you can see at a glance the time things need to be done each day. Students may also mention that they can see the week organized as a whole. Students should mention that the schedule will help them get to class on time because they can readily tell which classes follow each other.

Page 5: **1.** Band, JV Volleyball, Pottery **2.** No, because JV basketball starts at 3:30 and Drama club ends at 4:00.

3.	**Monday**	**Tuesday**	**Wednesday**	**Thursday**	**Friday**
2:30	Chess	Pottery	Homework Help	Pottery	Chess
3:00	Chess	Pottery	Homework Help	Pottery	Chess
3:30	JV	JV	JV	Student	JV
4:00	Basketball	Basketball	Basketball	Volunteers for	Basketball
4:30	Practice	Practice	Practice	Environment	Practice

ON YOUR OWN: Students should include necessary daily activities and fun optional activities.

Page 7: **Notes in Bulls column can include**: Points: 96 (circled); Pippen 26 pts. (starred); Jordan 23 pts.; Longley 16 pts and 12 rebs.; Rodman 18 rebs. (starred); Game went into OT. Bulls 19th straight win against Detroit (underlined). Longley back from hamstring injury. Bulls 45 - 25 rebound advantage over Pistons.
Notes in Pistons column can include: Points: 87 (circled); Hill 16 pts. Hill percentage low, 5 of 14 FGs and 6 of 11 FT (starred); Team's fifth game in seven nights (underlined).

Page 8: **Notes in Lakers column can include**: Points: 103 (circled). Starters: O'Neal, Jones, Van Exel, Campbell, Horry; Lakers led 30-26 at 1st qtr (underlined); Jones misses some important FTs (starred)
Notes in Jazz column can include: Points: 108 (circled). Starters: Malone, Stockton, Ostertag, Russell, Hornacek. Jazz win: Take 2-1 lead in playoffs (circled); Stockton makes two 3-pointers in a row (starred); Jazz led 55-49 at half; Malone 36 pts, 12 rebs. (starred)

Page 9: **2.** Penny Hardaway plays guard for the Orlando Magic. He's 26 years old, 6-feet-7 inches tall, and weighs 200 pounds. Penny is a spectacular passer and shooter. In 1995, his fourth NBA season, Penny was named to the All-NBA team and helped the Magic make it into the NBA finals. He was named to the All-NBA team again in 1996. Penny remains an explosive scorer. He recorded back-to-back 40-point games in the 1997 playoffs. **3.** Shaquille O'Neal plays center for the Los Angeles Lakers. He is 25 years old, 7-feet-1 inch tall, and weighs 301 pounds. Shaq is very big and strong and is virtually unstoppable in the lane. In his five-year NBA career, Shaq has won many honors. In 1993 he was named Rookie of the Year. During the 1994-95 season he led the NBA in scoring. Shaq was named one of the NBA's 50 greatest players.
ON YOUR OWN: Partners should be able to write clear paragraphs from each others notes.

ANSWER KEY (continued)

Page 11: **Underlined portion of the article can include:** Grant Hill; Detroit Pistons; entered the league in 1994; 1995-96 led NBA with 10 triple-doubles; Grant came out of Duke University; looking to fit in with Detroit Pistons, nothing more; it bothered him that because he led Duke to two NCAA championships people expected him to transform Pistons overnight; shy growing up, being a leader did not come easily; it all changed after being on the 1996 Olympic Dream Team; convinced him that he had the ability and personality to take charge of the Pistons. **1.** In 1994 **2.** Hill was shy growing up **3.** After the 1996 Olympics. Being on the Dream Team convinced Hill he had the ability and personality to take charge of the Pistons.

Page 12: **Underlined portion of the box score:** HAWKS: Blaylock 7 (assists); 80 (total pts.); Lauderdale, James, Neubill, or Recasner (fewest rebounds); PISTONS: Hill, 25 (pts.); 93 (total pts.) **1.** Pistons **2.** Hill **3.** Accept Lauderdale, James, Neubill, or Recasner. **4.** Blaylock

Page 13: **1.** power forward **2.** center **3.** shooting guard **4.** center **5.** small forward **ON YOUR OWN:** Answers will vary.

Page 15: **Almanac Title and Year:** Answers will vary; **1-6.** Answers will vary

Page 18: **1.** 4 **2.** adjective **3.** mongooses or mongeese **4.** halftime **5.** noun **6.** memorandums or memoranda **7.** A dish that is made from eggs and baked until puffed up. **8.** vapor **9.** necessary **10.** aspiring **11.** any of various flatfish; the undersurface of a foot

Page 19: **2.** saxaphones; 16 **3.** cameras; 3 **4.** Roosevelt, Eleanor; 15 **5.** zebras; 20 **6.** Arkansas; 1 **7.** presidents, U.S.; 14 **8.** Empire State Building; 6 **9.** Chavez, Ceasar; 3 **10.** the universe; 18

Page 20: **1.** C **2.** E **3.** F **4.** D **5.** B **6.** C **7.** E **8.** F **Page 21: 1.** c **2.** d **3.** S **4.** T **5.** A **6.** T **7.** S **8.** S **9.** S **10.** A

Page 22: **A.** Click on Cleveland Rockers Icon or red Schedule button at top; **B.** Click on red hypertext under Bullets Chat or the name Vicky Bullet red hypertext under photo or red Players button at top; **C.** Click on Charlotte Sting Icon or red Scores and Stats button at top; **D.** Click on red hypertext about Michelle Edwards under Cool as Ice or on red Players button at top; **E.** Click on red Tickets button at top; **F.** Click on red hypertext "Sign up for WNBA.com's What's NEXT?"

Page 23: **1.** c **2.** a **3.** a **4.** b **ON YOUR OWN:** Students should demonstrate that they can use research materials, including the Internet, and write a biographical paragraph.

Page 25: **1.** Philadelphia **2.** Atlanta **3.** Cleveland **4.** Go west on Interstate 10 until you get to Mobile. Go north on Interstate 65 until you reach Interstate 80/90. Go west on Interstate 80/90 to Chicago, IL. **3.** Go south on Interstate 95 to Boston. Go west on Interstate 90 until you reach Cleveland, OH.

Page 26: Students who follow directions and connect lines correctly will create a star shape on grid.

Page 27: **1.** Answers will vary for each student name. **2.** 27 should be circled; 32 should have an X; 28 should have an X **3.** 563 should be circled; 356 should have an X; 1,290 should be circled; 1,190 should have an X **4.** "enter" is underlined; (1) eaten, (2) either, (3) entrance; "lane" is underlined; (1) lend, (2) line, (3) long **5.** The row of numbers has an X, the column of numbers has a check; 141 is circled. **7.** Answers will vary. Possible activity: circle the car words underline the furniture words. **8.** Answers will vary. Possible activity: cross out the sports words, circle the food words then write a funny sentence using those words. **ON YOUR OWN:** Answers will vary.

Page 28: Student rating for each tip will vary. Students' own tip should demonstrate an understanding of how to improve their test-taking.

Page 29: Student answers will vary. Students responses on the chart should demonstrate that they can recognize realistic test-taking tips that will help them with their own studies.

Page 31: **1.** Auburn University **2.** eight years **3.** 1992 Olympics in Barcelona **4.** b **5.** b **6.** Answers will vary. Possible details include: **a.** He has made the All-NBA First Team five times; **b.** He's played in eleven straight All-Star Games; **c.** Only one of twelve players in NBA history to score over 19,000 points. **d.** He's scored 56 points in one game. **7.** Answers will vary. Some students may agree that it is a good idea to have a sense of humor in sports, while others may disagree with the idea.

Page 32: **1.** Students should complete and sign their pledges.

Turn young basketball fans into superstar students with Slam-Jammin' skills books from Scholastic and the NBA!

NBA Slam & Jam Math Skills

The only math books kids can't wait to get their hands on! These books teach math concepts such as multiplication and division, fractions, charts, graphs and statistics that will help raise grades and test scores.

Grades 3-4	ISBN: 06383-9	$2.95
Grades 5-6	ISBN: 06384-7	$3.50
Grades 7-8	ISBN: 18847-X	$3.50

NBA Slam & Jam Map Skills

These colorful, action-packed books teach vital geography skills such as direction, scale, latitude and longitude, time zones, and more!

Grades 3-4	ISBN: 06380-4	$2.95
Grades 5-6	ISBN: 06381-2	$3.50
Grades 7-8	ISBN: 18848-8	$3.50

NBA Slam & Jam Reading Skills

Kids will master the reading comprehension skills they need to be effective readers as they complete the attention-grabbing activities in these books.

Grades 3-4	ISBN: 06387-1	$2.95
Grades 5-6	ISBN: 06388-X	$3.50
Grades 7-8	ISBN: 18846-1	$3.50

NBA Slam & Jam Study Skills

Includes lessons, tips, and strategies to help students develop study skills that improve school performance. Topics include: getting organized, test taking, using reference sources, taking notes, using the Internet.

Grades 6-8	ISBN: 18849-6	$2.95

Call 1-800-331-4624 to order any of the titles listed above.

NBA
SLAM & JAM
STUDY
SKILLS

Using the Dictionary

How many times have you been told to "look it up?" Probably a lot, right? Obviously, you look up words in a dictionary to find out their meaning. But there are other reasons to look up words in the dictionary. The sample entry at right shows you some of the other reasons you might want to look up a word.

how a word divides into syllables

pronunciation

multiple meanings

other forms of the word

part of speech

pictures

al•le•giance (uh-**lee**-junss) ***noun*** Loyal support for someone or something.
al•ler•gic (uh-**lur**-jik) ***adjective*** If you are **allergic** to something, it causes you to sneeze, develop a rash, or have another unpleasant reaction. People can be allergic to dust, pollen, foods, and other things.
> ***noun*** **allergy** (**al**-er-jee)
al•ley (**al**-lee) ***noun***
1. A narrow passageway between or behind buildings or backyards.
2. bowling alley A long, narrow lane down which you roll bowling balls. Also the building where you go to bowl.
> ***noun***, **plural alleys**
al•li•ance (uh-**lye**-uhnss) ***noun*** A friendly agreement to work together.
al•lied (**al**-ide) ***adjective***
1. People or groups that join together for a common cause are **allied**. *The allied troops forced the enemy back across the border.*
2. Similar or related. *She'll take biology, chemistry, and other allied subjects.*
al•li•ga•tor (**al**-i-gay-tuhr) ***noun*** A large reptile with strong jaws and very sharp teeth, related to the crocodile. Alligators live in parts of North and South America and China.

alligator

Use your own dictionary to research and answer the questions below. If you need help locating the information, check the sample page at right.

1. How many syllables are in the word perspiration? ____________

2. What part of speech is the word civic? ____________

3. What is the plural of mongoose? ____________

4. Is the word written half time or halftime? ____________

5. What part of speech is the word fraction? ____________

6. What is the plural of memorandum? ____________

7. What is a souffle? ____________

8. What is the correct spelling, vaper or vapor? ____________

9. What is the correct spelling, necessary or neccessary? ____________

10. What is a synonym for ambitious? ____________

11. What are two definitions of the word sole?

a. ____________

b. ____________

Using an Encyclopedia

Yikes! You have to write a report on the history of basketball...by Monday. Where can you turn for help? (Assuming that you don't have Michael Jordan's telephone number!) The encyclopedia, of course! An encyclopedia will give you all the information you need.

The picture below shows an encyclopedia set. It has many volumes. Encyclopedia entries are organized alphabetically by topic or subject. A topic or subject is a general category or theme, such as "basketball" or "philosophy." For example, to find out about basketball you would look in the volume marked "B."

Use the set of encyclopedias below to answer the following questions. Write the subject that you think you would look up in the first space. Write the volume number where you would find that subject in the second space. We've done one for you.

1. What were the events leading up to the Civil War?
Subject Civil War **Vol.** 3

2. What is a saxaphone made of?
Subject ____________________ **Vol.** _____

3. How is a camera similar to a human eye?
Subject ____________________ **Vol.** _____

4. What are some of the details of Eleanor Roosevelt's life?
Subject ____________________ **Vol.** _____

5. How many different kinds of zebras are found in Africa?
Subject ____________________ **Vol.** _____

6. What is the capital of Arkansas?
Subject ____________________ **Vol.** _____

7. Who was the 26th president of the U.S.?
Subject ____________________ **Vol.** _____

8. How tall is the Empire State Building?
Subject ____________________ **Vol.** _____

9. Why is Ceasar Chavez an important figure in history?
Subject ____________________ **Vol.** _____

10. What do scientists know about the history of the universe?
Subject ____________________ **Vol.** _____

LESSON 5 RESEARCH TOOLS

Using the Library

Imagine you are researching a paper or a presentation on the history of basketball. Where will you find the information you need? The library is usually your best place to start. You may be familiar with the library's encyclopedias, but did you know the library has a whole lot more to offer? Take a look below at some resources you can find in a library. Then test your library skills by answering the questions.

A. Card Catalogs
This is the place where you can look everything up by title, author, or subject. These days, more and more libraries have their card catalogs on computers.

B. Shelves or Stacks
This is where a library's books are kept. To find shelved books, use the card catalog.

C. Vertical Files
These file cabinets hold pictures, photographs, brochures, pamphlets, and articles that don't fit on a shelf. They're stored in alphabetical folders.

D. Periodicals
You'll find newspapers and magazines here. To save space, older periodicals are often transferred to microfilm or microfiche. Use the periodical index to find the magazine you need. One index commonly used is the *Reader's Guide to Periodical Literature.* You can also use computerized databases to find a periodical.

E. Reference Books
Springfield, Massachussets is where basketball began. You can find Springfield in an atlas in the library reference section. Other reference books you might find there are encyclopedias, dictionaries, and almanacs.

F. Audio and video Resources
This is where CD's and videos are kept. Who knows? You might find a videotape of a past NBA great like Julius Erving or Kareem Abdul-Jabbar.

DON'T FORGET! The best library resource of all is your librarian. He or she will know how to help you find exactly what you need.

Which of the above library resources would you use to find information about the following topics? Write the correct letter of each resource in the blanks below.

_____ **1.** A brochure from the NBA Hall of Fame.

_____ **2.** The location of Salt Lake City, Utah, home of the Utah Starzz, a charter team of the WNBA.

_____ **3.** A recording of the radio broadcast of Wilt Chamberlain's 100-point game.

_____ **4.** An article about last year's playoffs.

_____ **5.** A biography of Shaquille O'Neal.

_____ **6.** An oversized photograph of John Stockton.

_____ **7.** A map of Philadelphia, home of the 76ers.

_____ **8.** A video about the history of basketball.

Working with a Card Catalog

Of course, the key to finding most of the things you need in a library is knowing how to use a card catalog. Almost all card catalogs work the same way. They list books alphabetically by:

- **Title** (the name of the book)
- **Author** (the person who wrote the book)
- **Subject** (what the book is about)

If the subject of the book is a person, the catalog lists him or her by last name. The same is true for authors. A "call" number, like the one on the sample catalog card below, shows you where the book is located in a stack.

call number — 796.323 Jordan, Godfrey — **author's name**
Hoops: The Complete Guide to Basketball and the NBA by Godfrey Jordan. Random House (Canada), 1995. — **book title**
number of pages — 155 p. illus
Descriptions and fun facts about basketball and the NBA. — **book subject**

Shaquille O'Neal of the Los Angeles Lakers

Use what you know about card catalogs to answer each question.

1. You'd look for Michael Jordan's autobiography in the card catalog
- ❍ a. by author, under "J" for Jordan
- ❍ b. by subject, under "J" for Jordan
- ❍ c. by either author or subject, under "J" for Jordan
- ❍ d. by author, under ``M" for Michael

2. To find *Hoops*, the book featured in the sample catalog card above you'd
- ❍ a. Look up your favorite authors to see if they've written about basketball
- ❍ b. Look up the subject "Basketball"
- ❍ c. Look up the title
- ❍ d. both b and c

Look at the list below. In the blank next to each item, write "S" for subject, "T" for title, or "A" for author.

3. ________ The NBA Finals

4. ________ *Slam Dunking the Easy Way*

5. ________ Coffey, Wayne

6. ________ *Dribble! Shoot! Score!*

7. ________ Basketball camps

8. ________ The WNBA

9. ________ Rebecca Lobo

10. ________ Layden, Joe

Using the Internet

Besides the library, another research tool you can use is the collection of computer networks known as the Internet. Using a computer linked to the Internet from home, school, or the library, you can gain access to information from all around the world. One part of the Internet is known as the World Wide Web. This web is a collection of pages — forms and documents — you can access with a software application called a browser. Whether you want to find out more about basketball's inventor, James Naismith, or the newest league around, the Women's National Basketball Association (WNBA), it's never a bad idea to head for the web. To learn more, take a look at this web page from the WNBA's site, www.WNBA.com.

Back/Forward
You can go back and forth between pages you have already downloaded using these two buttons.

URL or Uniform Resource Locator
Think of this as the "address" of the web page. Every page on the web has one.

Icon Links
On a web page, icons and logos can be links. To find out more about the Cleveland Rockers, for example, you could click on the Rockers logo.

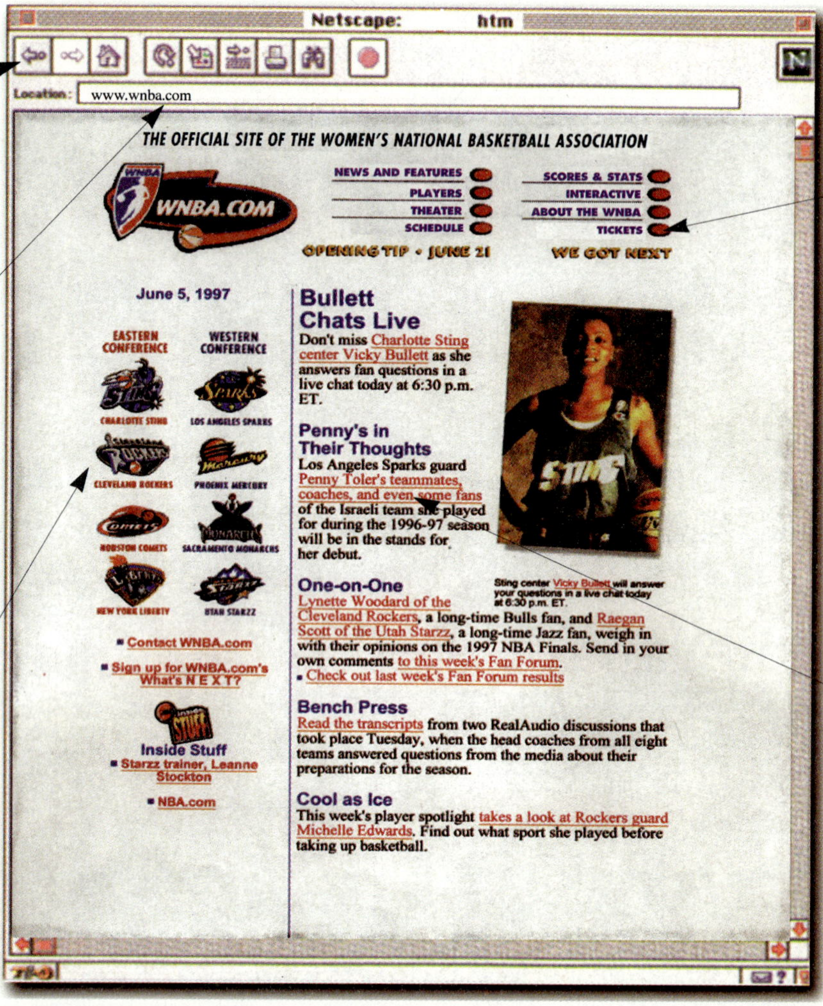

Button Links
A click here will take you to different pages with information about the subjects listed.

Text Links
The red underlined text (known as hypertext) indicates links. To find out more about Penny Toler, or to take a look at the Fan Forum, just point and click on this text.

Write each letter onto the web page above to show where you might click to find the following information. There might be more than one place you could click for each example.

A. The Cleveland Rockers' schedule.

B. Information about Sting center Vicky Bullett

C. The score of the most recent Charlotte Sting game.

D. Information about Rockers guard Michelle Edwards

E. Information about tickets to a game

F. To sign up for WNBA.com's "What's NEXT?"

Using the Web for Research

There are millions and millions of pages on the World Wide Web. If you don't know how to find what you want, it can be easy to get lost. The best way to find what you need is to use keywords to help your search. The right keywords can make the difference between a successful search and an unsuccessful one.

Suppose you wanted to find information on James Naismith, the inventor of basketball. If you just enter the word "basketball," you might get 30,000 results, too many to be useful. If you modify your search by entering more specific keywords like "basketball" and "inventor" you might get fewer than 30,000, but still too many. If you just enter the keyword "Naismith" you might get links to many WWW pages that include information about other people named Naismith, who don't have anything to do with the invention of basketball. If you enter the words "basketball," "inventor," and "Naismith," however, odds are you will find a manageable number of web pages with helpful information. Use the steps below to help you conduct a successful search.

1. Think carefully about the best keywords to use in your search.
2. To focus your search, use specific keywords about your subject. Eliminate broad keywords.
3. If you don't get many results, try adding more keywords.
4. Leave off suffixes or endings on long words. For example: instead of foul-shooting use foul shots.
5. Make sure you spell keywords correctly.

Circle the letter for the keywords that provide the best results for each search:

1. To find out about the Basketball Hall of Fame
a. hall of fame
b. fame basketball
c. basketball "Hall of Fame"

2. To find out about the WNBA's Charlotte Sting
a. basketball Charlotte Sting WNBA
b. Charlotte basketball
c. Charlotte

3. To find out if James Naismith wrote any books about basketball
a. "by James Naismith" basketball
b. Naismith basketball
c. books basketball James

4. To find out the Utah Jazz home schedule
a. home schedule
b. home schedule Utah Jazz
c. Utah home

On Your Own

Use the web site **WNBA.com** or library research tools to gather information about one player in the WNBA. Write a one-paragraph biography about that player's history and accomplishments.

Follow Me!

It's late in the fourth quarter and the Miami Heat are trailing by eight points. There's not much time left for them to come from behind and win.

So what does Heat Coach Pat Riley do? He calls for a time-out. Riley hopes he can give his players the necessary directions to come from behind and pull off a big win. He wants to tell them what plays to run, and who should get the ball for a shot. The Heat know they need to listen to Riley and follow his directions. Being able to follow directions is the only way any team can win.

Following directions is also an important skill to have in life. Your teacher gives you directions for assignments and tests. Your grades depend on how well you follow them. You can count on future bosses giving you directions for how they want a job done. Often, how well you follow those directions will affect how well you do in that job—especially when it's time for a raise or a promotion.

The activities on the next three pages will help you sharpen your skill at following directions. Before you go any further, here are three simple directions to get you warmed up.

1. Look at the titles of the activities on the next three pages. That way you'll know what you'll be working on.

2. Before you start each activity, read the directions carefully, so you'll know exactly what to do.

3. Finally, as you complete the activities, think about how following directions is an important skill for you.

Miami Heat center Alonzo Mourning

AMAZING NBA FACT

Alonzo Mourning is one of 49 children raised by foster parent Fanny Threet.

Getting to the Game

Imagine that you're an NBA official. To be a successful referee, you need to get to each game on time. That's why it's important to read and follow directions carefully.

Read each set of directions below. Use the map to help you figure out where you are and where you're going.

1. Start in Nashville, TN. Travel east on Interstate 81. Turn north on Interstate 77. Turn east when you get to Interstate 76. Continue to head east for about 400 miles. What NBA city will you be in?

____

2. Head north on Interstate 95 from Miami, turn west on Interstate 10. Continue to travel west till you get to Mobile. Head north on Interstate 65. Then turn northeast on Interstate 85. If you go about 200 miles on Interstate 85, what NBA city will you reach?

____

3. You've just spent the night in Frankfort, KY. The next morning you:

- Go west on Interstate 64
- Head north at Interstate 65.
- Head east on Interstate 90.

What NBA team will you be visiting?

____

How well can you give directions? Here's how to find out. Using the map, write the directions for these trips:

4. From Tallahassee, FL to Chicago, IL

____

____

____

____

5. From Portland, ME to Cleveland, OH

____

____

____

____

Following Directions—Accurately!

To get open shots and work together as a team, NBA players always have to follow directions. If each player listens to and follows the coach's directions, the team has a better chance of winning.

Below is a set of directions. If you follow them correctly, you'll create a picture with a special message. Use the grid square court below to draw your diagram.

1. Chicago Bull Michael Jordan is in square B1. Write MJ in the center of that square.
2. Teammate Scottie Pippen is in square C2. Write SP in the center of that square.
3. Utah Jazz point guard John Stockton is driving towards the basket. He's in square A2. Write JS in the center of that square.
4. 1997 MVP and Utah Jazz star Karl Malone is set to take a shot or grab a rebound. He's hanging out in square A3. Write KM in the center of that square.
5. Chicago Bull Luc Longley is ready for a breakaway pass in square C3. Write LL in the center of that square.
6. Now draw a line and connect the players' initials in this order: MJ, KM, SP, JS, LL, and then back to MJ. The shape you make will show what kind of players these guys are!

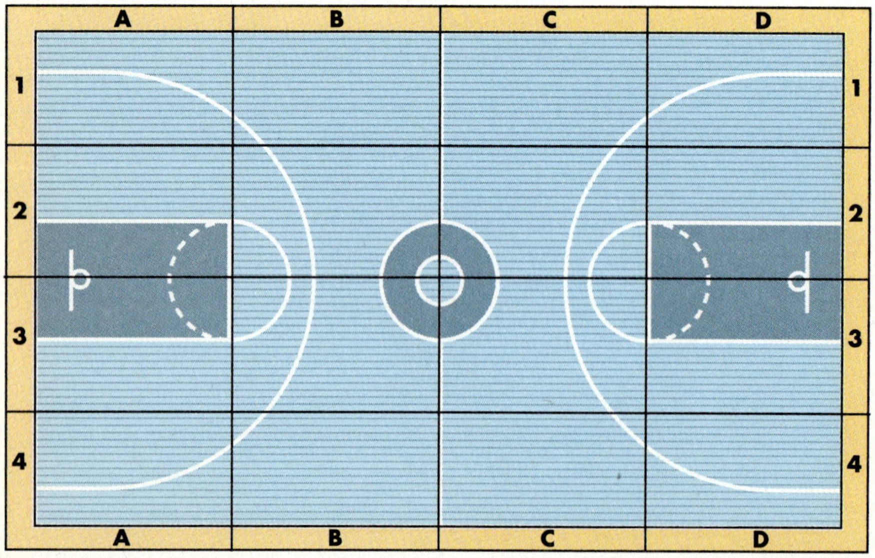

Michael Jordan of the Chicago Bulls

AMAZING NBA FACT

In the 47th NBA All-Star Game, Michael Jordan had 14 points, 11 rebounds, and 11 assists! He was the first player in All-Star history to record a triple-double!

Following Test Directions

All kinds of written tests have directions. The test directions say what the test taker must do. To do well on a test, you must follow the directions exactly.

Read these test directions below. Then do exactly what they say.

1. Print your last name inside the first row of boxes below. Print your first name in the second row. After that, leave one space blank. Then write your middle initial.

2. Look at the row of numbers in the boxes below. Circle the number of this page. Put an X on the number of the pages in this book. Put another X on the number of the page that Lesson 7 begins on.

22	23	24	25	26	27	28	29	30	31	32

3. Look at the numbers at the left of each row. In each row, circle the number that is the same as the number on the left. Then put an X on the number that is closest to, but not greater than the number on the left.

563	653	356	563	593
1,290	1,190	2,190	1,291	1,290

4. In each row below, underline the words that are the same. Then put the other words in the row in alphabetical order. You can do this by writing 1, 2, or 3, above the words.

enter	either	entrance	enter	eaten
lend	lane	long	line	lane

5. Complete the problems below. Then put an X in the box at the left of the row of numbers. Put a (✓) in the box for the column of numbers. Finally, circle the greater sum.

☐ 29
63
+ 49

☐ 22 + 6 + 80 + 4 =

Now try writing directions. Look at each set of words below. Design an activity for each set of words. Then write the directions for the activity on the lines provided. Try a set of directions that has more than one step. We've done the first one for you.

6. orange antelope lavender crayfish green

Circle the colors. Underline the animals.

7. trunk couch table radiator tires chair

____

____

8. basketball pizza salsa tacos soccer pasta

____

____

On Your Own

Have someone in your class try one of your activities. Can they follow your directions?

Practice Makes Perfect

It's playoff time in Orlando! Penny Hardaway, Horace Grant, and other Orlando Magic starters step onto the court. For them, each playoff series is a test. If they don't practice and prepare for the game, chances are they won't play well and win.

The same is true for you. Often how well you do on a test depends on how well you prepared for it. Take a look at the basketballs on this page. Each one has a tip that will help you prepare for a test. As you read each one, ask yourself, "Could this help me?" Use the scale at right and put a rating after each tip. Then, in the empty basketball, write your own tip to prepare for a test.

Rating Scale

1 really useful tip for r

2 somewhat useful tip

3 not a useful tip for r

1. Force yourself to begin studying early for a test. Waiting until the night before can be a disaster.
Rating: ☐

2. Use the questions in a chapter to help you study. If the book's author thinks the questions are important, your teacher probably will, too.
Rating: ☐

3. For math tests, try doing some problems from each of your homework assignments. If you can do those, you'll do fine on the test.
Rating: ☐

4. Sneak a few history or science vocabulary words into study hall each day. Learn them. Work with someone to memorize them.
Rating: ☐

5. Ask for help. There's nothing wrong with not understanding something. Most teachers will be glad to spend time helping you prepare for a test.
Rating: ☐

6. Before the test, try to get enough sleep. Also, eat well and avoid stressful fights with friends and family members.
Rating: ☐

Personal Tip

___

___

___

___

Test-Taking Survival Chart

Do you dread tests in some classes more than others? Do you know why? Use the chart below to help you think about the tests you have to take and how you can do better on them.

Penny Hardaway

To fill in the chart, follow these steps:

1. In the first column, list the classes whose tests you usually find difficult.
2. In the second column, write down the kind of test you usually get in that class (essay, multiple-choice, fill in the blank, etc.)
3. In the third column, write a tip, strategy, or plan for doing better on that test. (Check the tips on page 28 for ideas.)
   If you want, brainstorm with a classmate or friend to come up with a list of ideas.

Class	Kind of Test	Tip, Strategy, or Plan

One More Thing...

Of all of the tests that you listed on the chart, which one would you *really* like to do a better job in? Write that subject here: ______________________________.

One, Two, Three...Testing

If someone were to ask you how they could improve their rebounding skills, what would you tell them? You might tell them to practice. For some things, practicing is the only way to get better.

So if you want to get better at taking tests, how would you do it? **Practice** taking tests, of course. You can begin practicing right now by taking the test on these pages. Read the passage below and then answer the questions. As you complete the test, look for the helpful tips in blue along the way.

Sir Charles

He's been called "Boy George." He's been called "The Round Mound of Rebound." And he's also been called "The Leaning Tower of Pizza." Houston Rocket Charles Barkley has had many nicknames, starting way back with his basketball days at Auburn University in Alabama.

Now the explosive 6'6" forward is known as "Sir Charles" because of his success on and off the court. A joy to watch and listen to, he's become one of the game's leading ambassadors. He's had an extraordinary 12-year career, beginning with the Philadelphia 76ers in 1984.

"People sometimes get mad at me because I tell the truth," Barkley once said. "But anybody who knows me, I think, likes me. I'm a spontaneous person. My momma told me a long time ago to let my emotions out."

Charles Barkley was born February 20, 1963, in Leeds, Alabama. He was raised by his mother, a housekeeper, and his grandmother, a beautician. From the beginning, he always made people notice him.

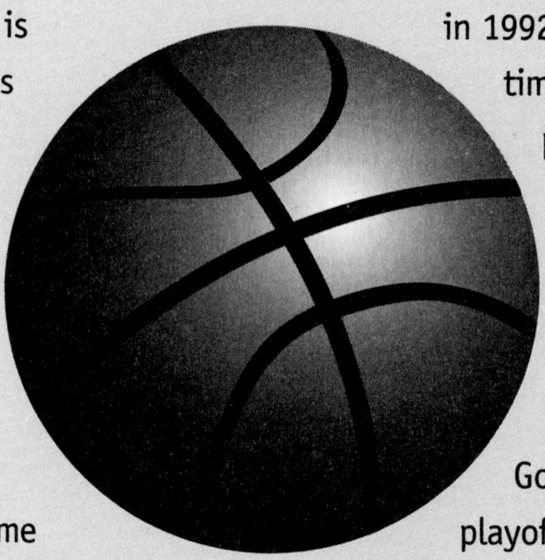

Barkley became Auburn's fourth all-time leading scorer. He was the fifth pick, taken by the 76ers, in the 1984 NBA Draft.

In 1986-87, he became the shortest player in league history to win the rebounding title. After eight years in Philadelphia and a gold medal performance as a member of the 1992 U.S. Olympic Dream Team in Barcelona, Spain, he was traded to the Phoenix Suns in 1992. In 1996, he was traded again, this time to the Houston Rockets, where he plans to end his career.

Injuries have limited Barkley in recent seasons, but he keeps coming back with key contributions when it counts — like his 56-point game against the Golden State Warriors in the 1994 playoffs. He made the All-NBA First Team five times and has been selected to eleven straight All-Star Games. He's one of 12 players in league history to score over 19,000 points.

Barkley's fierce desire to win is obvious to fans and players alike. But so is his sense of humor. The way in which he regularly pokes fun at referees, opposing players, and teammates, makes him one of the most colorful characters in sports.

How well did you read this article? Read and answer each of the questions below. The tips in blue will help you.

Some questions will check to see if you remember the details. If you can't remember an answer, scan the article again to find each detail.

1. Where did Charles Barkley go to college?

____

2. How long was Barkley with the Philadelphia 76ers?

____

3. When and where was Charles Barkley a member of the U.S. Olympic Dream Team?

____

____

Charles Barkley of the Houston Rockets takes it to the basket

Some questions will check to see if you understood what you read. If you aren't sure of the answer, slowly reread the part of the article that the question is talking about. Look for clues that might help you.

4. What does "spontaneous" mean?

❍ a. dishonest and careful

❍ b. without plan, effort, or thought

❍ c. shy and unhappy

5. What does the article mean when it says Barkley keeps coming back with "key contributions?"

❍ a. Barkley contributes keys to his team.

❍ b. Barkley puts in performances that make the difference between winning and losing to his team.

❍ c. Barkley is very generous with money.

6. What details support the idea that Charles Barkley is truly a great basketball player?

a. ______________________________

b. ______________________________

c. ______________________________

d. ______________________________

Some questions will ask for your own opinion on the topic. Don't be afraid to write what you think!

7. The last paragraph in this article refers to Barkley's sense of humor. Do you think it's a good idea to have a sense of humor in sports? Explain.

____

____

____

____

____

Now that you've completed this study skills book, you need to have a plan of action. A plan of action can help you set goals and use the skills you've just learned. Complete the plan below by checking the study skills you feel you need to work on. Then add an item of your own to the checklist. Sign the pledge and get ready for a whole new school experience!

My Study Skills Plan

______ I will budget my time by making a weekly schedule and sticking to it.

______ I will take careful, organized notes in class.

______ I will read assignments carefully and underline important points in books and articles I own.

______ I will use reference books such as dictionaries and encyclopedias to find the information I need.

______ I will take advantage of research tools I have available, such as the library and the Internet.

______ I will listen to and carefully follow all directions, especially test directions.

______ I will study and prepare as best I can for every test.

✔ I will... ______________________________

____

____

I, ______________________, promise to carry out this plan of action to the best of my ability.

______________________________ ______________

(Student's signature) (date)

______________________________ ______________

(Parent or teacher's signature) (date)